KT-432-667

THE HISTORY AND TECHNIQUES
OF THE GREAT MASTERS

BRUEGEL

Penelope Le Fanu Hughes

TIGER BOOKS INTERNATIONAL
LONDON

A QUARTO BOOK

This edition published by
Tiger Books International Ltd
3, Friars Lane,
Richmond,
Surrey, TW9 1NL

Copyright © 1989 Quarto Publishing plc
All rights reserved. No part of this publication
may be reproduced, stored in a retrieval system
or transmitted in any form or by any means,
electronic, mechanical, photocopying, recording
or otherwise, without the permission of the
copyright holder.

ISBN 1 85501 013 5

This book was designed and produced by
Quarto Publishing plc
The Old Brewery, 6 Blundell Street
London N7 9BH

Project Editor Hazel Harrison
Designer Carole Perks
Picture Researcher Katherine Russell-Cobb

Art Director Moira Clinch
Editorial Director Carolyn King

Typeset by Aptimage Limited
22 Clinton Place, Seaford, East Sussex BN25 1NP
Manufactured in Hong Kong by Regent
Publishing Services Limited
Printed in Hong Kong by Leefung-Asco
Printers Ltd

CONTENTS

INTRODUCTION

Pieter Bruegel The Elder
(artist unknown)
c 1569

"On his journeys Bruegel did many views from nature, so it was said of him when he travelled through the Alps that he had swallowed all the mountains and rocks and spat them out again, after his return, onto his canvases and panels, so closely was he able to follow nature here and in his other works." The quotation is from Karel Van Mander's *Het Schilder-Boek (The Painter's Book)* published in 1604, thirty-five years after Pieter Bruegel's death. It is still a major source of information on his life, about which very little is otherwise known. Our knowledge of the career of this much-reproduced artist has to be built around this biography and reinforced by some mentions in contemporary documents and letters and Bruegel's own work, which is frequently signed and dated.

Van Mander's vivid description of Bruegel's interpretation of nature was in fact extremely apt, for it was through a series of landscape drawings, published as engravings soon after his return from a long journey to Italy, that Bruegel first became known. His later paintings of the *Months* (see pages 43 and 47), which fuse landscape and keen observation of human activity in a way that was totally new in the 16th century, are among his most memorable images.

Although Van Mander described many of Bruegel's paintings accurately, he characterized the artist himself as a somewhat droll and peasant-like person, which does not accord with other accounts. Two contemporaries of Bruegel — the Italian Ludovico Guiccardini, who published a *Description of the Low Countries* in 1567, and Dominico Lampsonius, a poet, painter and historian from Liège — described him as a second Hieronymus Bosch. The latter (who died in 1516) was still famous, and the comparison was a compliment as well as being to some extent accurate. Bruegel drew on Bosch's imagery for some of his paintings and for the subject matter of the many popular engravings designed for the leading Antwerp print publisher, Hieronymus Cock. Van

Mander's view of him is unfounded: modern scholarship has shown that he was in fact connected with a highly intellectual circle in Antwerp, which included the great geographer and cartographer Abraham Ortelius and other leading figures of the time, such as the publisher Christopher Plantin.

Apprenticeship and formative years

Pieter Bruegel's birth date is not precisely known and nor is his place of birth, but it is generally thought that he was born towards the end of the 1520s in Breda, Northern Brabant, in the modern Netherlands. In 1551 he became a Master in the Antwerp Guild of St Luke (the painter's guild) meaning that he had completed his training as a painter, and during this year he collaborated with an older painter named Pieter Baltens on an altarpiece in Malines. This town was at the time a centre for tempera painting on linen, a technique which Bruegel later used for several paintings. Van Mander tells us that Bruegel's actual apprenticeship was with Pieter Coecke van Aelst (1502-50) a distinguished and intellectual Antwerp artist who had travelled in Italy and Turkey and who ran a large workshop producing tapestries and sculpture as well as paintings. Although Bruegel's early work in no way resembles Coecke's Italianate style, the fact that he was later to marry Coecke's daughter confirms a connection.

Although Bruegel's work does not initially show reliance on the Italian style, he would have been keen to travel to the South, as were all aspiring Northern painters. In the 16th-century Netherlands, Italy was regarded as the source both of the admired style of the Italian Renaissance and of the world of antiquity from which the Renaissance in part derived. Prints after the work of Italian masters were widely circulated, and by Bruegel's day earlier visitors to Italy, such as the painter Frans Floris, had absorbed the Italianate figure style based on Raphael and Michelangelo, while Maerten van Heemskerck had made drawings of ancient Roman

PIETER COECKE VAN AELST
The Resurrection of Christ
date unknown, Staatliche
Kunsthalle, Karlsruhe

This painting, the central
panel of a triptych, gives an
idea of Coecke's Italianate
style. Like other leading
Flemish painters of his day, he
was strongly influenced by
Raphael and his school.

Coecke, who visited Rome,
was active as a painter from
1527, first in Antwerp and
later in Brussels. According to
Van Mander, he was also
Bruegel's teacher, but this is
not substantiated by any
document, and Bruegel's early
paintings in no way resemble
those of Coecke. Coecke died
in 1550 and Bruegel married
his daughter in 1563.

monuments and sculpture which were engraved in Antwerp.

Dated drawings and records show that Bruegel made the vital journey between 1552 and 1554, visiting Lyons in France and then going on to Italy — to Reggio in Calabria, Messina and Palermo in Sicily, to Naples, Rome and possibly Bologna. In Rome he met the famous miniaturist Giulio Clovio (to become the patron of El Greco). Clovio was later to own four paintings by Bruegel, including one of Lyons (probably a tempera painting on linen) and a painting on ivory — presumably a miniature — of the Tower of Babel, a subject Bruegel was to use again for two large paintings. It was probably also in Rome that Bruegel produced in 1553 his first dated painting, *Christ Appearing to the Apostles at the Sea of Tiberias*. Its high viewpoint and pointed rock formations recall the work of two earlier Flemish landscape painters Joachim Patinir (d. 1516) and Herri met de Bles (c 1500/10-after 1550).

Landscape and the role of printing

On his way back from Italy Bruegel spent a considerable time in the Alps making landscape sketches. The drawings, which reveal keen observation and a sensitive handling of the shapes and textures of mountains and trees, were to furnish motifs for later compositions such as the series of large landscape drawings on which he worked when he returned to Antwerp. These, engraved by Hieronymus Cock, demonstrate his outstanding mastery of landscape composition.

In the prosperous city and port of Antwerp with its large international population — by 1550 it numbered 100,000 people — pictures and prints were big business. Guiccardini describes the traffic in oriental spices, grain, French wines, German metals and English cloth, as well as the prosperous picture market in the centre of Antwerp. Three hundred qualified masters were at work; pictures were often purchased sight unseen before delivery, and whole cargoes were despatched to Spain. Printing was an equally important activity; more than half the books published in the Low Countries were printed in Antwerp, and there was a thriving trade in prints, which were exported to all parts of Europe and imported from Italy and Germany. Hieronymus Cock had established his large publishing house, the Four Winds, in about 1550, and was a leading printer. He produced a variety of subjects, including maps and topographical scenes, as well as prints after leading Netherlandish and Italian masters.

Since the beginning of the century there had been an important tradition of landscape painting in the Netherlands. The Alps were then just beginning to be explored, and it is possible that it was Cock who had encouraged Bruegel not only to go to Italy but to record the Alpine landscape with a view to creating the large-scale engravings which he now produced after Bruegel's drawings. The landscapes are not topographical records of actual places, but a skilful mixture of motifs drawn from Bruegel's own on-the-spot sketches. These were blended with imaginative ideas, some of which look back, as Bruegel's first landscape painting had done, to Joachim Patinir's rocky landscapes and to the sweeping panoramas introduced by Herri met de Bles.

Patinir's concept of a
panoramic landscape,
surveyed from a high
viewpoint, had already
appeared in the work of an
earlier Flemish artist, Hans
Memling. But Patinir is the
first known landscape
specialist. In this tiny panel,
one of his few signed works,
the figures of the holy family,
dwarfed by towering rocks,
are less important than the
landscape stretching away to
its far horizon. Patinir had
many immediate followers,
the principal one being Herri
met de Bles, and was an
important influence on
Bruegel.

Bruegel's graphic work

In 1556 Bruegel began work on satirical or moralizing figure compositions, also intended for engraving by Cock. The first of these was based on a well-known proverb, "Big fish eat little fish." Proverbs, and a delight in categorizing aspects of the world's folly, were endemic to the Netherlands of this period. *Ship of Fools* (1494), by the German scholar Sebastian Brandt, a satirical comment on contemporary folly and vice, was well known, as was Erasmus's *In Praise of Folly* (1509), which had many themes in common with it. As early as 1500 Erasmus had published a collection of Greek and Latin proverbs, and the first Netherlandish collection appeared in 1549. Bruegel's subject was one which everyone would have known.

The drawing shows a huge fish, mouth gaping, with its inside split to reveal a myriad of increasingly smaller fish inside it. The boat and the human beings in the foreground emphasize the size of the biggest fish. The engraving made from the drawing extends the meaning of the proverb, with a legend printed in Latin, French and Flemish: "Oppression of the poor; the power of the rich controls you." Cock published this engraving as "designed by Hieronymus Bosch," perhaps capitalizing on Bosch's enduring popularity to ensure its success; Flemish painters such as Jan Mandyn and Pieter Huys had already produced paintings in Bosch's style in the previous decade, while the great collector Cardinal de Granvella — later to be a patron of Bruegel — com-missioned tapestries after his work. Bruegel was to follow the Bosch fashion in some of his paintings, and also in the series of drawings of the Seven Vices and the Seven Virtues, which he now produced for engraving by Cock.

The conflict between vices and virtues had been used by the medieval Church to teach moral lessons, and cycles personifying them were common in medieval art. In the *Allegory of Lust,* from the Seven Vices series, Bruegel represented Lust as a nude woman being caressed by a half-lizard, half-human creature. The rotting tree beneath which they shelter is topped by an embracing couple in a transparent bubble set into a half-open mussel shell, both motifs which appear in Bosch's *Garden of Earthly Delights.* Just below, a branch turns into an antlered stag, traditional symbol of sexual passion, while on the left two dogs echo the central couple (an idea which re-appears in a more restrained form in William Hogarth's *Marriage à la Mode* of 1743). The large-headed monster in the foreground breaks an egg (regarded as an aphrodisiac at the time) over himself. Bruegel's fantastic creatures, like Bosch's, are a mixture of animal, bird, and human parts extended by straight invention, the kind of creations which were to fill his later painting *The Fall of the Rebel Angels* (see page 27). The subject matter, style and composition of Bruegel's graphic work are often echoed or extended in his paintings and a knowledge of it contributes enormously to our understanding of him.

PIETER BRUEGEL
Country Concerns (Solicitudo Rustico)
c 1555, British Museum, London

This beautiful drawing, in pen and ink over black chalk, is the only surviving preparatory work for the series of engravings known as *The Large Landscapes*. Its composition resembles the part-imaginary landscapes of Joachim Patinir, but the sensitive draughtsmanship reflects Bruegel's careful study of the real world. Note the delicate, tentative outlines of river and mountains, the variety of strokes used to differentiate rocks, trees and buildings.

The influence of Bosch

In parallel with his work for Cock, Bruegel was also producing paintings, and *The Netherlandish Proverbs* of 1559 introduced a new compositional device — a village setting viewed, like the landscapes, from high up. This is also used for *The Battle between Carnival and Lent* (see page 19) and *Children's Games* (see page 23). These paintings combine some of the weirdness and drollery of Bosch with Bruegel's own amazing eye for recording the multifarious activities of human beings, also demonstrated in his figure drawings, sometimes inscribed *nar het lieven* (from the life).

Two years later Bruegel's painting becomes more obviously Bosch-like with *The Fall of the Rebel Angels, Dulle Griet* and *The Triumph of Death*. In the latter Bruegel sets his scene of the living battling against the dead in a vast landscape luridly lit by flaming fires. The concept recalls the Northern theme of the Dance of Death, where the dead rise from their tombs, dance and go off to find new victims among the living. There is also

PIETER BRUEGEL
Landscape with the Fall of Icarus
c 1555, Musée Royaux, Brussels

At one time it was thought that this painting had been done on wood and then transferred to canvas, but laboratory examination has now shown that canvas was the original support. Bruegel had worked at Malines, a centre for tempera painting on canvas, in 1550. The work is undated, but is usually considered to have been produced around 1555 after his return from Italy, although there is now some degree of doubt as to whether the painting is by Bruegel.

PIETER VAN DER HEYDEN
(after a drawing by Pieter
Bruegel)
Big Fish Eat Little Fish
1557, British Museum, London

Although the original design was by Bruegel, the publisher Cock had the words "Hieronymus Bos—inventor" (left-hand corner) added to help sell this engraving. The word ECCE (behold) was also added to draw attention to the contrast between the soldier tackling the biggest fish and the ordinary man freeing a small one. The soldier's enormous knife carries the Christian symbol of the orb and cross, suggesting that dealing with evil must involve spiritual as well as human strength. On the bank a fisherman supplies the antithesis to the main subject: he uses a small fish to catch a bigger one.

a parallel with the Italian Triumph of Death, where three living princes encounter three dead ones. Bruegel could have seen such paintings on his Italian journey. It is interesting to consider this picture in the context of the troubled state of the Netherlands at the time. The country had been ruled since the beginning of the century by governors appointed first by the Holy Roman Emperor, Charles V, and then (from 1555) by Philip II of Spain, and increasing measures against religious heresies (i.e. non-Catholic) were provoking local resentment. But there is no evidence to link his portrayal of sacking and looting with contemporary events, and Bruegel himself was a Catholic. Perhaps it is more apt to view the picture as a powerful and universal statement about the helpless-

ness of humanity in the face of the inevitability of death.

In 1563 Bruegel moved to Brussels, where he married Mayken, the daughter of his former teacher Pieter Coecke. He continued to work there until his death, both on paintings and on designs for Hieronymus Cock. His first son Pieter, who also became a painter (Pieter Bruegel the Younger), was born in 1564, by which time Bruegel had produced two versions of *The Tower of Babel* (see page 31), a subject he had already treated in Rome several years earlier. As well as showing extraordinary understanding of the complex construction of an intricate building, the painting exhibits a new tenderness in the delicate treatment of light and shade in the landscape background, presaging the profound revelation of

PIETER BRUEGEL
Allegory of Lust
1557, Bibliothèque Royale, Brussels

This small drawing was engraved by Pieter van der Heyden and published by Cock in the *Seven Deadly Vices* series. Bruegel's debt to Bosch can be seen in the way the pictorial field is crammed with variations on the same theme (in this case Lust). The rotting tree trunk and other "love pavilions" dotted around, and the fountain of love in the distance, derive from Bosch's *Garden of Earthly Delights* and, ultimately, from the famous medieval love garden described in the 13th-century allegorical poem *The Romance of the Rose*. The couple making love in the centre parody the seduction of Adam by Eve as seen in 15th century engravings.

landscape in the later paintings of the *Months* (see pages 43 and 47).

The later religious paintings

In 1564 three religious paintings underline the variety of Bruegel's painterly conceptions. The large *Procession to Calvary* (see page 35) combines vivid observation of contemporary manners with large foreground figures derived from early 15th-century Flemish painting; *The Adoration of the Kings* (see page 39) shows his awareness of the elongated figures of 16th-century Mannerism, while *The Death of the Virgin,* painted for his friend Abraham Ortelius in *grisaille* — with greyish tonalities worked on a yellowish background — is notable for its subject matter. This necessitated an interior setting, unique in Bruegel's painting, and the subtlety of its light effects anticipate those of Rembrandt. *Grisaille,* or monochrome painting, had been used in Flemish painting since the 15th century, often on the wings of altarpieces, and was a technique Bruegel also used for a small

panel of *Christ and the Woman taken in Adultery,* which he kept with him until he died.

The subject of the Virgin's death as presented in the painting was derived from the 13th-century *Golden Legend* of Jacobus de Voragine, who wrote an account of the patriarchs, confessors and holy virgins present at the Virgin's death. This is supposedly recorded in an apocryphal book of St John the Evangelist, who is shown in the left foreground of the painting with eyes closed as though imagining the miracle of the resurrection. Four separate sources of gentle light — including the candle which according to an old custom is being placed in the hands of the dying Virgin, its light a symbol of Christian faith — are dimmed by the radiance which flows from the Virgin herself. The painting can be seen as a triumphant statement of belief in Christian salvation. In 1574 Ortelius had it engraved for some of his friends, one of whom, the poet and engraver Dierick Volckhertzoon Coornhert, testified to the power of Bruegel's art when he wrote from Haarlem to thank Ortelius. "I examined it

HIERONYMUS BOSCH
The Garden of Earthly Delights
(central panel)
c 1505-10, Prado, Madrid

Bosch, intensely religious, produced both altarpieces and moralizing works, such as this painting, packed with the symbolic subtleties that appealed to contemporary Flemish taste. The scene — a garden of lust rather than love — forms the centre of a triptych, and is flanked by depictions of the Garden of Eden and Hell. Many of Bruegel's paintings look down in the same way on a panorama crowded with small figures, and his *Allegory of Lust* includes specific details from this composition. Probably executed for a lay patron, *The Garden of Earthly Delights* was eventually acquired by Philip II of Spain.

with pleasure and admiration from top to bottom for the artistry of its drawing and the care of the engraving . . . methinks I heard moaning, groaning and screaming and the splashing of tears in this portrayal of sorrow." Other letters from Ortelius's intellectual friends also bear witness to the high esteem in which Bruegel was held.

Bruegel's other *grisaille* panel, *Christ and the Woman Taken in Adultery* (stolen from the Courtauld Institute Galleries, London, in 1982) can be interpreted as a plea for religious tolerance, an attitude endorsed by Abraham Ortelius and others in his circle. Some of the figures in the painting, particularly that of the woman turned towards Christ, show an Italianate style, and can be related to the famous cartoons designed by Raphael in 1515-16, which could have been seen by Bruegel in Brussels, where they had been sent for weaving. These figures pave the way towards the more monumental style which Bruegel was to adopt in his later paintings.

New departures

Another characteristic belonging to many of the later paintings is an increasing interest in movement which Bruegel had already shown in the small *Landscape with*

the Flight into Egypt of 1563 (Courtauld Institute Galleries, London). This painting is one of the few that can be precisely traced to the prestigious collection of Cardinal de Granvella, who in 1560 had been created archbishop of Malines and appointed by Philip II chief counsellor to the regent of the Netherlands, Margaret of Austria. Granvella's regard for the unrestricted authority of the monarch led to conflict with the freedom-loving group that emerged under the leadership of William of Orange in 1564. Forced to leave the Netherlands and his art collection, he is recorded as being particularly worried about his Bruegels.

PIETER BRUEGEL
The Netherlandish Proverbs or
(The Blue Cloak)
1559, Staatliche Museen,
Berlin-Dahlem

Over eighty-five popular proverbs are acted out here, and acts of folly spread out to the horizon where three tiny figures represent the parable

of the blind. Spiritual blindness and the foolishness of the world is further emphasized by the orb and cross held by the seated Christ. An elegant man (foreground) balances it on his thumb and indicates the cripple who can't see it for looking. It reappears on the inn upside down.

PIETER BRUEGEL
The Triumph of Death
c 1562, Prado, Madrid

Vividly rendered incidents of
death and disaster are backed
by a smoke- and flame-filled
landscape. Skeletons toll the
bell of death (left); high
wheels holding rotting corpses
(a contemporary reference),
and in the left-hand corner a
falling ruler cannot stay a
looting skeleton. On the right,
a woman stumbles before a
cartload of skulls drawn by an
emaciated horse. The skeleton
with a scythe represents death
cutting life short, and the
horse he rides — almost a
skeleton itself — is the red
horse of war described in the
Book of Revelations.

The new feeling for movement and the increasing
ability successfully to combine figures and landscape
culminated in the large paintings of the *Months* which
Bruegel produced for the Antwerp banker, Niclaes
Jonghelinck, in 1565. Using a combination of superb
landscape panoramas, acutely and sympathetically
observed figures, and a palette chosen in each case to
epitomize the major colours of the season depicted,
Bruegel achieved a presentation of landscape which was
completely new in its evocation of atmosphere and its
seemingly close relation to nature. His way of painting
also changed, shifting from the more precise execution
of earlier works to a rapid, spontaneous — sometimes
almost sketchy — technique, with the paint often applied
quite thinly and the underpainting sometimes left visible. This is a technique that the great 17th-century
Flemish painter Rubens, who owned several Bruegel
paintings, obviously studied closely.

The years between 1566 and 1569 saw the continued
production of both paintings and drawings by Bruegel
and the birth of Bruegel's second son Jan (in 1568), who
was to become a still life and landscape painter. Bruegel's
paintings were as varied as ever in both subject matter
and approach, ranging from biblical subjects to peasant
scenes and proverbs and from dazzling landscape panoramas to close-ups of monumental figures. The *Peasant
Wedding* (see page 55), *The Parable of the Blind* (see page
59) and *The Conversion of St Paul* are among the prod-
ucts of these years. According to Van Mander, Bruegel
was also commissioned by the City Council of Brussels to
do a series of "pieces" celebrating the construction of the
new Brussels-Antwerp canal, but he died in 1569 before
they could be done.

This was a period which saw an increase in the
hostility felt in the Netherlands for the ideas of Philip II.

Although William of Orange had succeeded in removing Cardinal de Granvella, a request in 1564 for the withdrawal of the Inquisition (established in the Netherlands since 1522) and of the more rigorous anti-heretical edicts was countered by the arrival in 1567 of the Spanish Duke of Alva, who established a reign of terror. Van Mander says that Bruegel had his wife destroy some of his drawings before he died because they were "too biting and sharp" and might have brought her trouble. This may or may not be true; it is unlikely that any of Bruegel's paintings of these years was intended to reflect current events, but it is possible that his modern-dress presentations of subjects such as *The Numbering at Bethlehem* (see page 51) and *The Massacre of the Innocents* might have been seen by contemporaries as a general comment on governmental restrictions and an endorsement of the growing demands of the Protestants for freedom from persecution.

Bruegel died in September 1569, and his wife Mayken in 1578. They were buried in the church in which they had been married, Notre Dame de la Chapelle in Brussels. It was there that their son Jan put up a memorial to them adorned with a painting of *Christ Giving the Keys to St Peter* by Rubens, a fitting tribute from the

next great Flemish painter and perhaps a reminder of Bruegel's personal faith and belief in spiritual salvation. While that can only be guessed at, Bruegel's paintings — totalling less than fifty and mostly produced between 1555 and 1569 — remain as an incontestable and vital testimony to his personal vision and technical brilliance. They are as fresh and exciting today as they must have been in the 16th century, and their indefinite capacity for interpretation only serves to underline the richness of the genius that created them.

PIETER BRUEGEL
The Death of the Virgin
1565, Upton House (National Trust), Banbury, Oxfordshire

Bruegel painted this tiny *grisaille* panel (only $14\frac{1}{2} \times 22$ inches/36×55 cm) for his friend Abraham Ortelius. Although it was engraved

after Bruegel's death its tonal subtleties make it unlikely that it was designed with engraving in mind. The almost palpable reverence and sorrow which emanate from the mourning group epitomize Ortelius' words about Bruegel — that "he painted many things that cannot be painted."

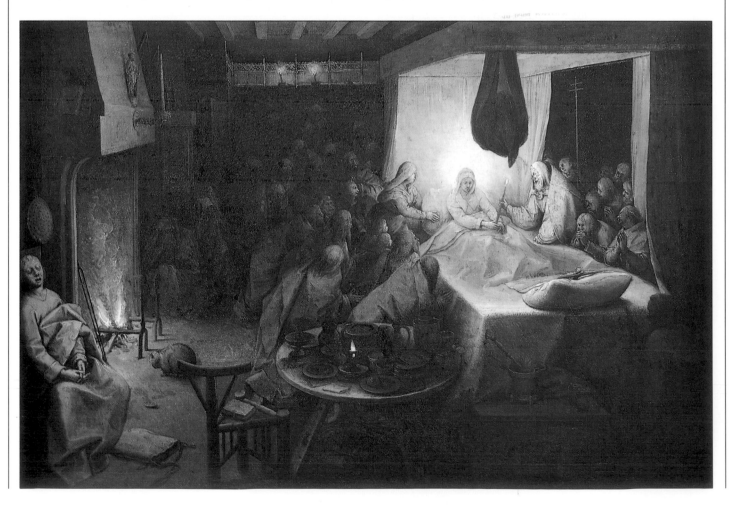

BRUEGEL'S PAINTING METHODS

This detail from *The Tower of Babel* shows both Bruegel's amazing skill in rendering architectural detail and the variety of his brushwork.

The luminous effect of light in the background of *The Procession to Calvary* is the result of successive applications of thin glazes over a white gesso ground.

In this area of *The Adoration of the Kings* Bruegel's underpainting can be seen because the top layers of paint have thinned with age.

Bruegel was heir to the finely detailed techniques found in 15th-century Flemish painting, most of which, like his own, was in oil on wood panel. The panels for painting were made to order by specialist joiners from seasoned oak, probably imported from Poland. They were then prepared for painting, first being planed as smooth as possible and then covered with layers of a whitish ground made of chalk mixed with animal glue. The ground filled up any remaining unevenness in the wood and formed a foundation on which subsequent areas of colour could be built up.

The next stage was to sketch out the final composition in an underdrawing (similar to the *sinopia* of a fresco). Bruegel's underdrawings (now visible through infrared photography and reflectography) were made with a thin paint line. They are particularly interesting because they show that he often changed his mind between a first and a final idea. A few extant drawings are evidence that he also worked out ideas on paper. Once the underdrawing was established it was covered with an intermediate layer, probably of size or underpaint, before the actual painting was begun. For the final stage, pigments were ground up, mixed with linseed oil (and possibly turpentine) and applied, often quite loosely, in thin layers. Details and highlights were added in tiny strokes, and Bruegel sometimes gave emphasis to his figures by delicately outlining them."

The brilliant reds and glowing orange-browns in paintings such as *A Peasant Wedding* are the result of the slow, careful technique of building up layers of thin paint over an underdrawing. Such brilliance is difficult, indeed almost impossible, to achieve with the opaque, buttery paint used by most oil painters today.

All pigments were ground by hand before painting, usually by apprentices or assistants, and the range of colours used was relatively small. Those used by Bruegel would have included the following:
Dark blue — azurite (apparently difficult to obtain because it had to be imported from Hungary, which was repeatedly invaded by the Turks).
Mid blue — smalt (used as a substitute for azurite and made from blue cobalt glass)
Green — malachite (green copper pigment)
Yellow — ochre and lead-tin yellow
Red — vermilion (a sublimation of sulphur and mercury)
White — lead white prepared by artificial means

CHRONOLOGY OF BRUEGEL'S LIFE

Late 1520s Pieter Bruegel (the Elder) was probably born sometime between 1525 and 1530 in Breda, North Brabant.

1551 Bruegel becomes Master of the Guild of St Luke in Antwerp after an apprenticeship with (according to his biographer Karel Van Mander) the Antwerp painter Pieter Coecke van Aelst.

1552-4 Travels in France and Italy, visiting Lyons, Calabria, Sicily, Naples, Rome and possibly Bologna. Returns over the Alps. Works for the miniaturist Giulio Clovio while in Rome, and it is probably there that he paints in 1553 his first signed and dated painting: *Christ Appearing to the Apostles at the Sea of Tiberias.*

1555 Returns to Antwerp, where he lives until 1563. Produces only surviving drawing for the *Large Landscapes*, engravings published by Hieronymus Cock. Probable date of painting *Landscape with the Fall of Icarus.*

1556 Drawing for the print *Big Fish Eat Little Fish* published by Cock as the work of Hieronymus Bosch.

Children's Games

The Fall of the Rebel Angels

The Corn Harvest

1556-9 Works on drawings for engravings of *The Seven Vices* and *The Seven Virtues*. Paints *The Battle Between Carnival and Lent* (1559).

1560 Paints *Children's Games.*

1562 Paints *The Fall of the Rebel Angels.*

1563 Paints *The Tower of Babel.* Moves to Brussels, where he lives for the rest of his life. Marries Mayken, the daughter of Pieter Coecke van Aelst, and continues to produce designs for Hieronymus Cock.

1564 Birth of son Pieter (the Younger), who was also to become a painter, and frequently copied his father's work. Paints *The Procession to Calvary* and *The Adoration of the Kings.*

1565 Paints the cycle of the *Months* for the Antwerp banker Niclaes Jonghelinck.

1566 Paints *The Numbering at Bethlehem.*

1567 Probable date of *The Peasant Wedding.*

1568 Birth of second son Jan, to become a still life and landscape painter, sometimes called Velvet Bruegel. Paints *The Parable of the Blind.*

1569 Death of Bruegel in Brussels.

1578 Death of Bruegel's wife.

The Parable of the Blind

THE PAINTINGS

THE BATTLE BETWEEN CARNIVAL AND LENT

signed and dated 1559
46½×64¾in/118×164.5cm
Oil on panel
Kunsthistorisches Museum, Vienna

In the foreground of the painting is the confrontation between feast and fast — figures representing Carnival (on the left) and Lent. This had already been the subject of a print by the Malines artist Franz Hogenberg, published by Hieronymus Cock the year before, and was a concept that might have been acted out in villages during the Carnival season. It was also the theme of plays produced by the *rederijker kamers* (chambers of rhetoric) which existed in most Netherlandish towns, and which performed plays and organized the allegorical floats used in religious processions. At the centre of the scene a couple led by a jester — every *rederijker kamer* had one — underlines the *rederijker* connection and, by extension, the theme of the world as a stage.

Carnival, portrayed as a pot-bellied man, sits astride a barrel jousting with a spit loaded with rich meats, while the thin, sad figure of Lent is armed only with a griddle displaying two small fish — suitable Lenten fare. Carnival is crowned with a rich game pie; Lent wears a beehive surrounded by busy bees symbolizing (since St Ambrose) the Church and its Community. A broader comparison fills out the painting with the sweep of Carnival celebrations on the left and pious Lenten observances on the right. Two men gamble in the extreme left corner; a group in front of the inn watches a popular play, *The Dirty Bride*. This tells the story of a peasant who aped the ways of the rich — the hero is leading his untidy bride to the marriage bed inside a rickety tent. The inn sign with the words "In the Blue Boat" refers to the name of societies which organized Carnival festivities — but the phrase "Blue Boat" was also used to describe people who wasted their time on drinking and gambling. In front of the building behind the inn, another play, *Urson and Valentine* (the story of two twins separated at

birth but finally reunited), is being performed while a procession led by bagpipers files up the street.

In contrast to the mindless revelry on the left, whose participants ignore the group of cripples in their midst, the crowd behind Lent is dutiful; the children's foreheads are marked with the penitential ash of Ash Wednesday, the first day of Lent; beggars are rewarded with alms; there is plenty of trade at the fish stall, and a group of people carrying chairs, showing they have just attended a sermon, comes out of the church. In contrast to the inn's sign, the church's trefoil window recalls the Trinity, while statues below its arch are already suitably draped for Lent.

Bruegel does not seem to favour one side more than the other, although he ensures that the main subject comes over clearly by making the figures of Carnival and Lent proportionately larger than all the others, an old-fashioned device which makes sense of the packed scene. One detail might indicate a deeply spiritual comment: the trees in the background are lightly greened in contrast to the bare branches behind the Carnival side, and it is tempting to read the greening as symbolic of the new life that believers would find reaffirmed in the Resurrection of Christ on Easter Sunday. But it is more likely to denote the passage of time: the practices of Carnival and Lent do not actually coincide, as here, but succeed one another. At the centre of Bruegel's stage the jester, like the shepherd in *Landscape with the Fall of Icarus,* may be the clue to the underlying meaning of the painting. He leads towards the Carnival side of the painting, but the directions of the footsteps of the couple behind him — one to the left, one to the right — suggest both the eternal uncertainty of humanity and the possibility of choice between good and evil.

The high viewpoint, revealing a village setting crowded with figures, was also used by Bruegel in *The Netherlandish Proverbs* painted in the same year and in *Children's Games* of 1560 (see page 23). All three paintings can be related compositionally to Bosch's *The Garden of Earthly Delights* (see page 11), from which Bruegel had borrowed motifs for the engravings of *The Seven Vices* (1557). The concept of a world of absurd happenings spread out before the spectator as though on a stage can be connected with the idea of the *Theatrum Mundi* (Theatre of the World), derived from Classical antiquity and current in 16th-century thought.

1 *Actual size detail*

1 *Actual size detail* The coat of the man with the mandolin is painted in a delicate range of tones from the pale pink highlighting his pot belly to the subtle darks used for creases and folds. These tonal changes are made smoothly, while a different treatment is used for the garment of the clown-faced woman behind — tiny parallel brushstrokes of contrasting light and dark indicate the rough texture and structure of the material, possibly fur. Dark outlines applied with a fine brush to faces, fingers and legs make these details stand out from a distance.

2 Bruegel has noted the contrasting light effects created by the glow of the flames on the broadly sketched figures around the fire and by the brightly lit doorway which throws the standing figures into relief. The architectural details of the houses above are precisely delineated; even the inset brick arches over the windows are suggested by controlled flicks of paint.

3 In this area of the painting six cripples exhibit their deformities. The one in the centre is dressed up in a paper hat and has fox tails dangling from his cloak. The attitudes of the figures are clarified by dark outlines, and particular attention is paid to the cast shadows of the crutches. Thinly applied paint on garments and on the areas between the figures shows the underpaint and the underlying texture of the original chalk and glue ground.

2

3

CHILDREN'S GAMES

Signed and dated 1560
$46\frac{1}{2} \times 63\frac{3}{8}$ in / 118×161 cm
Oil on panel
Kunsthistorisches Museum, Vienna

Portraying as it does more than ninety contemporary children's games, the painting was probably designed to appeal to the passion for cataloguing and classifying human behaviour characteristic of Humanist cultures. Like *The Netherlandish Proverbs* (see page 12) and *The Battle Between Carnival and Lent* (see page 19) this scene would have been attractive to the Humanist collectors and scholars in Antwerp with whom Bruegel was associated.

Again the painting has a high viewpoint, and the world spread out before us shows over 200 children briskly engaged in diverse activities: hoop-rolling, playing knucklebones, leapfrogging, spinning tops, walking on stilts and so on. The games are portrayed with a precision that resulted from Bruegel's perceptive observation and drawings of the natural world and its inhabitants. As such, they are enjoyable just to look at, but deeper meanings can be looked for.

An anonymous poem published in Antwerp in 1530 had compared humanity with children who run and jump and fool around. The painting, like *The Netherlandish Proverbs*, could thus be generally symbolic of folly, an interpretation which can be supported in various ways. The strongly indicated diagonals of the composition meet just where two children are turning upside down on a bench, suggesting a topsy-turvy world where foolishness is rampant. The large mask displayed at the upper window on the left suggests "playing at masks," but also represents the tragedy or folly of life itself. The marriage procession with a child dressed as a bride is a focal event; it draws attention to a 16th-century literary tradition which saw marriage as foolish because it permitted lust and meant that woman would eventually be dominated by man.

Other aspects of the painting introduce another concept: the idea that playing is connected with learning. Parallel to the picture plane, and so dominating the town square, is an important building, probably the town hall, seat of local authority and a reminder of the civic virtues to which children's upbringing should ideally lead. And while summer games go on within the delicately painted landscape on the left, the long street on the right takes the viewer to a distant horizon — possibly representative of the larger world into which the children will inevitably pass.

Finally, there are two interesting games which balance each other at each corner of the foreground. On the left is knucklebones, the game of chance which can suggest that all life is a lottery; on the right there is a girl playing at shop, a game which involves the artist himself. The funnel and scales on the girl's bench are to measure the red dust she is scraping from the brick in front of her, and this was used to make a special artist's pigment. When Bruegel's famous predecessor, Albrecht Dürer, visited the Netherlands in 1520-21, he bought some of this pigment, and noted in his diary that Antwerp was its exclusive source because it was made from new red bricks unique to the town. Bruegel has placed his own name and 1560, the date of the painting, at the end of the bench containing the precious dust. This could be a deliberate reference to his special role as the painter and visualizer of another version of the Theatre of the World and its spectacle of the absurdity of human life.

Mentioned in Karel Van Mander's account of Bruegel's life, *Children's Games* was one of the paintings which eventually passed into the collection of Archduke Ernst of Austria (Governor of the Netherlands 1593-95) toward the end of the 16th century. Artistic precedents for the subject already existed in calendar miniatures and in series of the Ages of Man. The latter interpretation has been suggested in connection with this painting, but is unlikely in view of the fact that there are no records of any other paintings by Bruegel which could have formed part of such a series.

1 *Actual size detail*

1 *Actual size detail* Horizontal strokes of blue, pale blue and white, used for the water, contrast with the grassy areas where Bruegel has brushed on subtly mixed greens with varied brushstrokes, some vertical, some curved. Tiny strokes of darker greens are used for the reeds growing by the water's edge. The figures are simplified, but the girls' skirts include carefully placed shadows to give them volume and movement. The standing figure on the right is playing "whom shall I choose?"

2 Bruegel is following the laws of aerial perspective as he gradually diminishes the strength of colour with which he depicts the buildings in the street. Details and figures get smaller as they move further away from the spectator's eye. Yet the clarity of detail is not lost; the tiny figures are clearly seen playing "follow my leader," "hare and hounds," "piggy-back" and other games.

3 The big wooden beam that serves as a bench is painted thinly in dark brown dragged over a lighter tone to suggest graining. But the figures are painted in quite thick rich paint, with details such as the hanging laces of jerkins and the highlights on hands added in with tiny strokes of paint. Bruegel has signed his name on the end of the bench. Until 1559 he had spelt it "Brueghel," but then changed it, for no known reason, to Bruegel.

2

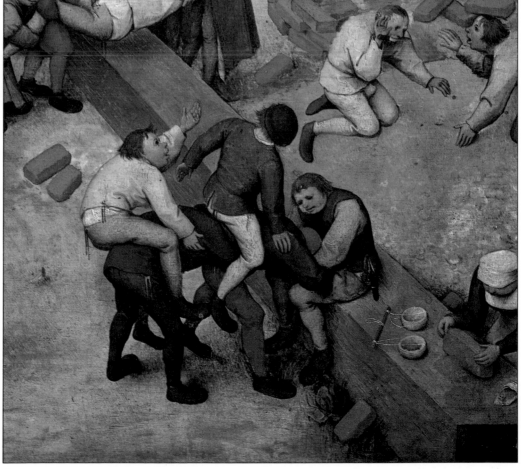

3

THE FALL OF THE REBEL ANGELS

1562

46×63¾in/117×162cm

Oil on panel

Musées Royaux des Beaux-Arts, Brussels

Some years earlier Frans Floris had painted a huge upright altarpiece of this subject in Italianate style, but Bruegel is closer to Bosch in this visualization of St Michael and his assistant battling against the rebel angels who, become the forces of Satan, turn into nightmarish figures as they fall. According to the early Church the creation of man was preceded by the fall of Satan, and in medieval and early Renaissance art the angels were shown falling from heaven. In the 16th century, the theme was merged, as here, with the war in heaven, the conflict between good and evil personified by the archangel Michael and Satan, the dragon. The battle is described in Revelations (12:7-9): "And now war broke out in heaven, when Michael and his angels attacked the dragon . . . known as the devil or Satan . . . The great dragon . . . was hurled down to the earth and his angels were hurled down with him."

Bruegel dramatizes the action-packed subject by bringing it so close that we look up to St Michael in the centre and can almost touch the contorted devilish creatures below. St Michael, originally the guardian angel of the Hebrew nation, but representative in a Christian context of the Church militant, is presented as a thin, elongated armour-clad figure raising a sword in his right hand while he protects himself with a shield marked with a cross. To each side two angel assistants, dressed in white albs, deal confidently with the swarms of weird creatures around them. Albs symbolize the robe of mockery with which Herod caused Christ to be clothed and the joy of those redeemed through Christ. In addition, the stole worn by the angel on the right is crossed over his breast as it would be when used as a vestment at Mass, perhaps suggesting that the forces for good must work through the Christian Church in the battle against evil. Bruegel follows the text of Revelations closely, for the quotation mentioned earlier continues: "Then I heard a voice shout from heaven 'Victory and power and empire for ever have been won by our God, and all authority for Christ now that the persecutor . . . has been brought down'."

Beside and below the three sword-bearers the changed rebel angels fall helplessly downwards. Satan, represented as the seven-headed dragon of Revelations, is shown already beaten down. The dragon's curving tail is uppermost beside St Michael, its heavy body and huge clawed feet leading downwards to its heads, identified by coronets and with eyes that look more bemused than terrifying. In fact all the vanquished creatures, though horrific, have an air of helpless surprise as if they do not quite know what has happened to them.

Bruegel uses a background ranging from blue-white at the top to dark tones at the bottom to represent the fall from heaven to earth. The serene trumpetting angels at the top are similar to the angels in much earlier 15th-century Flemish works, but Bosch is the prototype for Bruegel's amalgamation of different bits of things to make the fantastic beings: a human head combined with butterfly wings, a bodiless head with distorted arms, cat-like, fish-like, frog-like and bird-like creatures all defined with superb skill in the rendering of different textures and expressions. Bruegel had used similar creatures in his designs for the Seven Vices but made their action more restrained and placed them in a landscape setting. The violent action and extreme close-up of *The Fall of the Rebel Angels* is new in Bruegel's work, and forms a powerful visualization of the triumph of good over the forces of evil.

The date of this painting, 1562, was probably also the year in which Bruegel produced *The Triumph of Death* and a *grisaille* drawing of *The Resurrection of Christ*. These are subjects which relate to the final destiny of the human soul and of mankind in general, as does this painting, which is concerned in part with the depiction of the tortures of hell which supposedly awaited those who did not find their place in heaven. Initially the composition seems extremely complex, but the diagonals set up by the fallen angels, bottom left and right, which meet at a point directly above St. Michael's head, provide an element of stability.

1

1 Pink, golden-yellow and white give the angels a light airy feeling in contrast to the dark silhouette of the falling devil at the top. The angels' gestures are forceful, and their powerful wings are well-observed, with carefully drawn feathers and pinkish tips. The angle of the cross held by the lower angel helps to give a feeling of depth, and the curved trumpet on the left is highlighted to emphasize its curve.

2 The freely painted head of this monster is thrown into relief by the light paint of the area behind it. Its eyeballs are made to protrude by means of carefully placed highlights and its pointed teeth shown up by the dark interior of its mouth. Its hair is rendered with soft, loose brushstrokes and its crown — slightly askew — with light, delicate touches of paint. The underpaint and the texture of the ground can be seen beneath the thin paint on the face.

3 *Actual size detail* The beasts with crowns on their heads are part of the seven-headed dragon described in Revelations, which here represents Satan. Bruegel has used dark red-brown over lighter paint to suggest the depth and texture of their fur and the long mane of the lower beast. Sharp dabs of white are used for the pointed teeth and the highlights of the eyes. The intricately detailed crowns are rendered with dots and squiggles of paint. In contrast, a scrawny arm is emphasized with a dark outline, while dots of pale paint on the red sleeve of the trumpeter's raised arm enhances the brilliant colour.

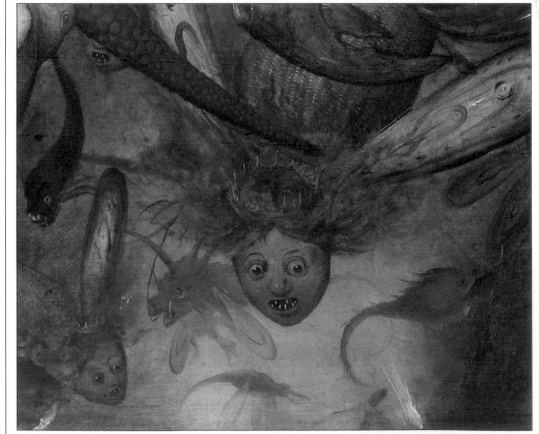

2

3 *Actual size detail*

THE TOWER OF BABEL

Signed and dated 1563
44⅞×61in/114×155cm
Oil on panel
Kunsthistorisches Museum, Vienna

The building of the tower of Babel is described in the Old Testament (Genesis 11:1-9). The descendants of Noah baked bricks and built a town, and a tower with its top reaching heaven, on a plain in the land of Shinar (Mesopotamia). God then punished the people's pride in their achievement by muddling up the common language that they spoke, so that they could no longer understand one another, and scattered them over the earth. The physical origin of the tower was the ziggurat, a large brick temple-tower which was a real feature of the ancient cities of Mesopotamia where Babel (Babylon) was located. Babel is described in the Bible as part of the empire of Nimrod (a legendary ruler of the second millennium BC), and the 1st-century Jewish historian, Flavius Josephus, expanded the account of the building of the tower to suggest that Nimrod had actually supervised it, as in this painting.

The subject had been treated by earlier Flemish artists, and one composition, which Bruegel could have known, uses all the same details: the group of people around Nimrod, the ships and the landscape. In Bruegel's version the crowned ruler, elegantly clad in a fur-lined cloak and holding a sceptre, appears in the left-hand corner; the workmen who have seen him are either down on their knees in front of him, or hastily getting onto them. Bruegel uses the figures, the houses round the base of the tower and the subtly lit landscape to emphasize the tower's enormous size, and he gives both the workmen and the town a realistically contemporary appearance which makes a telling contrast to the fantasy of the tower.

The tower itself is inspired by Bruegel's memories of the Colosseum in Rome and by prints of Roman ruins produced by the printer and publisher Hieronymus Cock, which Bruegel would have known. It shows a masterly understanding of building construction; the layered arches and the buttresses look completely believable, as do the various winches which are hauling up the big building blocks. The tower has an inner core built of red brick, but it is faced with creamy coloured stone, as were the great buildings of ancient Rome.

Making the tower reminiscent of ancient Roman buildings is a reminder that although they had been built to last for ever they had fallen into ruins. The tower is thus a symbol not only of pride punished, but also of the transience of man's earthly achievements. Literary comments echo such interpretations: Nimrod had been picked out in Dante's *Divine Comedy* as an example of punished pride, and writers contemporary with Bruegel used the ruins of Rome as an example of the fleetingness of man's work.

Bruegel produced three versions of this subject: this one, which was at one time owned by the Antwerp banker Niclaes Jonghelinck; a version on ivory painted for Giulio Clovio when Bruegel was in Rome; and a second smaller panel painting. The latter is usually thought to be dated about a year later than this, which it resembles except for the substitution of a contemporary stone quarry for Nimrod and his group.

This subject allowed Bruegel to display his amazing skill in rendering complex architecture in precise detail — a skill that lends support to Karel Van Mander's statement that Bruegel was asked shortly before his death to produce work celebrating the construction of the new Brussels-Antwerp canal. But the painting is also memorable for the way in which the landscape, with its intermittent sun and shade, catches the essence of the light of the Low Countries. In this respect, the picture anticipates the Dutch landscape painters of the 17th century, such as Jacob van Ruisdael.

1 *Actual size detail*

1 *Actual size detail* Swirling dark strokes are used to indicate the roughly hewn steps up the side of the living rock on which the Tower of Babel is being built. Minute traces of dark brown, creamy brown and white create the figures — more than forty of them in this area alone. The brick structure being erected is painted in reddish brown with minuscule marks in black and yellow to indicate detailing. Very thin strokes of dark paint are used to draw the ladders and poles against the luminous sky.

2 Amidst the crowded roofs of the town Bruegel has inserted tiny light patches of yellow and pale brown, anticipating the subtle light effects of 17th-century Dutch landscapes. The reddish brown of the houses are darkened to set off the grey-green of the castellated town entrance whose walls and arches are echoed by reflections in the sea. In the foreground of this detail Bruegel has shown how a large crane is worked by including the two men who are turning it from the inside, as if on a treadmill.

3 The sharp angled shapes of the blocks of marble show a delicate range of cream to grey tones. In some of the shadowed areas the brush marks are clearly visible. The rounded figures of the two stone-masons are painted in contrasting grey-green hues that pick up the colours of the ground on which the blocks are positioned. Tiny white highlights emphasize the tops of the pointed punches that are being used together with mallets to work the stone.

2

3

THE PROCESSION TO CALVARY

Signed and dated 1564

$48\frac{3}{4} \times 66\frac{7}{8}$ in/124×170 cm

Oil on panel

Kunsthistorisches Museum, Vienna

The subject of the procession to Calvary was familiar in Northern painting: there are versions by Herri met de Bles, Pieter Aertsen and others. The grieving foreground figures provide a moving commentary on the scene, and also introduce a diagonal which leads across to the high, Patinir-like rock, through the tiny figure of Christ struggling under the cross. The device of making the key figure very small is something Bruegel had used in earlier paintings such as *Landscape with the Fall of Icarus* (see page 9) and *The Battle Between Carnival and Lent* (see page 19). But once the figure of Christ is found it can be seen that he is linked with the holy figures in the foreground by the timeless garments they wear — all the figures in the crowd, including Simon of Cyrene, who is refusing to help carry the cross, are in 16th-century dress. This, and the fact that Bruegel includes rich details of contemporary life — such as the two thieves attended by priests or monks who are jolting along in a cart, the high wheels on which bodies were left to rot, and the general air of festivity that would have attended a public execution in the 16th century — point up the contrast between the crowd which is unaware of the significance of the event and the figures of the Virgin, St John and the two Marys who are deeply aware of it. Of the figures in the crowd, only the woman immediately behind the right-hand kneeling figure is grieving, and by turning towards the holy group, she makes a connection for the viewer.

Bruegel distances the foreground figures still more from the crowd not only by making them large but by modelling them on earlier 15th-century work, as he had previously done for the principal music-making angels in *The Fall of the Rebel Angels* (see page 27). They are particularly akin to the mourning figures in Rogier van der Weyden's *Descent from the Cross* (opposite below). This painting was no longer in the Netherlands at this time, but Bruegel could have known it from copies or from preliminary drawings for a print published by Hieronymus Cock. The print features a structure similar to the building with a bulbous dome visible in the blue-green background to the left of the large rock. Being completely un-Netherlandish, it represents the Temple at Jerusalem. The oddly placed windmill, where wheat would have been ground, may have been intended as a symbol of the Eucharistic bread, and taken together with the mourning group, would emphasize the true religious meaning of the scene and the lack of spiritual awareness evidenced by the crowd.

Bruegel's use in the foreground of a style derived from earlier Flemish work may have reflected a growing interest in the 15th century on the part of both painters and their patrons. The existence of the print after *The Descent from the Cross* is evidence of this interest, as is the fact that Domenico Lampsonius — who later wrote a poem about Bruegel — was corresponding in about 1559 with the Italian art historian Giorgio Vasari. He supplied details of both earlier and contemporary Flemish painters for the second edition of Vasari's *Lives of the Most Excellent Painters, Sculptors and Architects*, which was to appear in 1568.

This is one of the paintings that was owned by Niclaes Jonghelinck, who may even have commissioned it, and it is one of the few works for which known preparatory drawings for some of the

ROGIER VAN DER WEYDEN
The Descent from the Cross
c 1438, Prado, Madrid

figures exist. It is the largest of Bruegel's panels, and its combination of prominent foreground figures with a packed crowd scene against a landscape background is new, looking forward to the combination of large figures and landscape which Bruegel was to use for the paintings of the *Months* in the following year. Also new is the greater emphasis on movement, seen in the running people and the red-jacketed soldiers who sweep in a great arc towards Golgotha.

1 *Actual size detail*

1 *Actual size detail* This detail demonstrates Bruegel's acute observation. He differentiates between the stolidness of the onlookers and the liveliness of the standard bearer, and also between the plodding gait of the brown horse pulling the cart and the prance of the skewbald horse behind. Very thin paint is used for the hooves of the horse in the water and for the reflection of the man in red seated on the cart, and traces of white describe the water splashing up. Although this group is in the middle distance rather than the foreground, Bruegel has expressed the different emotions of each face with economy and precision, placing small, accurate marks for eyes, noses and mouths.

2 Bruegel has used very small brushes and a range of subtle colour gradations derived from the then conventional landscape colours — brown, blue, and green — to achieve the effect of distance. The blue-greens melt into each other, contrasting with the golden, turreted walls of what, in the context of the painting's subject, has to be the city of Jerusalem. The three-tiered domed building representing the temple is an imaginary structure, but the other buildings would have been those that Bruegel saw around him in his own time and country.

3 Pale green and brownish yellow was brushed on first, with the figures built up over it. Christ has been dramatically silhouetted against the diagonal of the cross. Its texture is rendered with tiny dabs of mixed greys and cream, the greys toning in with Christ's robe.

2

3

THE ADORATION OF THE KINGS

Signed and dated 1564
43¾×32¾in/111×83.5cm
Oil on panel
National Gallery, London

The composition of *The Adoration of the Kings* is Italianate, and the elongated figures are related to Mannerist painting, but Bruegel's overall presentation of the scene is completely unidealised, in contrast with traditional renderings of the subject. The position of the Virgin recalls the mourning Virgin in *The Procession to Calvary* (see page 35), while the pose of the Christ-child has been compared with that in Michelangelo's sculpture of the *Madonna and Child*.

Bruegel uses particularly rich colour in the foreground, and organizes his design around two strong diagonals. The dangling sleeve of the kneeling Caspar and his sheathed sword on the ground start a directional movement which continues through the Christ-child and Mary to the head of Joseph. A crossing diagonal set up by the fold of the standing king's coat leads to the crowd pressing in from the top right-hand corner of the panel. The closeness of the figures gives Bruegel the opportunity to render textures and material with considerable detail: the intricate folds of Mary's cloak are indicated in a rather sketchy way, but those in Joseph's sleeves and in the elaborate red jacket (note the triangular buttons) of the king on the left are carefully studied. But it is in the rendering of the various reactions to the central event that Bruegel shows particular mastery ranging from the sympathetic gaze of the man in black on the left to the radiant wonder of the standing king.

There are some unusual details, one being the gossip whispering into Joseph's ear — perhaps a query relating to Mary's purity which could have formed part of the content of a contemporary mystery play. Another is the presence of the soldiers with their upright spears and halberds: the halberd immediately above Mary could be interpreted as a reference to the crucifixion and the soldiers as a reference to the massacre of young children which is shortly to be carried out at the instigation of Herod. The ass in the background, without the ox usual in Nativity scenes, could thus be a reminder of the holy family's flight into Egypt to escape this persecution. This inclusion of elements which forecast events to come is seen again in *The Numbering at Bethlehem* (see page 51), where the ox is included along with the ass to indicate the forthcoming birth of Christ.

As is usual in paintings of this subject, the gifts brought by the kings are magnificent. At this time Antwerp was the most important centre of the goldsmith's art in the Netherlands, and the intricate way in which the gifts are painted suggests they could have been actual objects. The gold ship enclosing what looks like a nautilus shell would, if real, have been a very special piece. It could also be read as a reference to the tradition by which the Church was compared with a ship in which the faithful were borne to salvation.

This is Bruegel's only upright panel painting, and the first work to consist only of figures, many of them presented in close-up. The Magi, wise men from the East according to the Gospel account (Matthew 2:1-12) had been defined as three kings by early Christian writers, and their names originated still later. The oldest is Caspar offering his gift of gold, homage to Christ's kingship. Balthasar, the African, and Melchior bring gifts of frankincense (homage to Christ's divinity) and myrrh (used in embalming and so a foreshadowing of death). The kings represent the first manifestation of Christ to the Gentiles, and as such were associated in the Western Church from the 4th century on with the Feast of the Epiphany (Greek for manifestation) celebrated on January 6.

1 Underdrawing is very obvious on the chalice, and also shows the original positioning of the king's left hand, which was changed in the final version. The vessel is richly detailed, with yellow-brown and tiny thick white highlights. The king's face also shows traces of underdrawing and is less smoothly painted than the face of the Virgin. Shadowed areas are indicated with tiny lines of paint, rather than being modelled in tone, and the king's straggling hair is indicated with loose brushstrokes.

2 Blue underpaint can be seen above the foot, with traces of a thin layer of cream over it. Bruegel evidently changed his mind about the exact positioning of this foot, which was finally painted in richly applied orange-red with a line of dark shading beneath and round the heel.

3 *Actual size detail* Traces of underdrawing in blue paint can be seen here going from the Virgin's chin and curving round her breast. They are also visible on her left hand and on the arms and legs of the child, while squiggly lines of underdrawing can also be seen on his lower thigh. The final creamy coloured paint applied to the child's body shows that Bruegel rethought the composition here; it does not follow the underdrawing exactly. The paint on the Virgin's headdress is thin and also shows the underdrawing beneath, but is finished with quite thick flicks of white.

2

3 *Actual size detail*

THE HUNTERS IN THE SNOW

Signed and dated 1565
46×63¾in/117×162cm
Oil on panel
Kunsthistorisches Museum, Vienna

This arresting winter landscape is one of a series of paintings of the *Months* commissioned by Niclaes Jonghelinck, a rich Antwerp banker and a royal official. The paintings were designed as part of a large decorative scheme for Jonghelinck's town house, to which Frans Floris, the most successful Antwerp artist of the time, had also contributed.

The idea of a series of the *Months* was not new. It derived from the Labours of the Months often sculpted on medieval churches and illuminated in the calendar pages of psalters and books of hours. One of the most famous books of hours, the *Très Riches Heures,* created by the Limbourg Brothers for the Duc de Berry in the 15th century, represents some of the months by outdoor labours set in landscape. By the 16th century this approach had filtered into the Netherlands, appearing in both woodcuts and tapestries designed for domestic decoration.

The way in which Bruegel dealt with the concept was completely new, however, for he made the landscape and its atmosphere rather than the beautifully observed seasonal activities the real subject of each painting. It was also a new departure for Bruegel to make landscape paintings of this size; he had previously used large panels only for religious or allegorical subjects, crammed with lots of figures and activity.

Bruegel's series, which was finished by February 1566, probably consisted of twelve paintings, one for each month, but only five remain. In addition to this painting, representing January, there are *The Gloomy Day,* February, *Haymaking,* July, *The Corn Harvest,* August (see page 47) and *The Return of the Herd,* November. All five are similar in general composition, with large figures placed in the foreground and a landscape which stretches away behind them. This pattern would have suited the way in which the pictures were probably hung — high up on partially panelled walls, as was the fashion of the time. The landscape background of each painting would have provided a continuous sequence depicting the changing seasons of the year. Both composition and content make *The Hunters in the Snow* one of the most powerful evocations of winter ever painted. The hunters, thickly clothed against the freezing air and accompanied by their tired dogs, trudge wearily in from the left-hand corner of the painting. Their steady forward movement is emphasized by the receding line of still, snow-laden trees which leads the eye diagonally into the picture across the iced-up flooded fields and on to the harsh mountains thrusting up through the snow.

Bruegel completed the series within about a year, so he must have worked quickly — which points up the practised ease with which he conveys atmosphere and acutely observed action. His mountains look back to the imaginary landscapes of Joachim Patinir as well as to his own landscape drawings made in the Alps around 1554. The actual composition recalls his *Landscape with the Fall of Icarus* (see page 11): although much smaller, it has a similar high viewpoint and a diagonal which divides the main figures in the foreground from the landscape, as does the snow line in this painting.

The Hunters in the Snow created a type of winter scene which was to be echoed in later centuries, and is frequently reproduced in our own time. But it is not as carefree as it appears at first glance: the diagonal thrust of the composition leads straight to the chill of ice; the sky suggests more snow to come; only one of the hunters has an animal slung on his pole. Reminders of the harsh realities of peasant life are inexorably present in Bruegel's thrilling and timeless celebration of winter.

There are few extant drawings by Bruegel that can be identified as studies for a particular painting, but this appears to have a relationship to *Hunters in the Snow.*

1 Strands of white, yellow and red paint describe the flaring fire being used for pig singeing. The deep blackness of the figures crouched over the flames makes the snow appear more brilliant by contrast. The inn sign, crusted with snow and an icicle, reads "Dis is In den Hert" ("This is in the heart"). This could be a reference to St Hubert, patron saint of hunters, who is shown as a haloed figure kneeling in front of a stag. (The legend tells how he was converted, when hunting on Good Friday, by the sight of a stag with a crucifix between its antlers.) Interestingly, the inn sign hangs crookedly on one hook, which could be interpreted as one of Bruegel's many comments on humanity's lack of spirituality.

2 *Actual size detail* A restricted palette of brown, grey-green and white with touches of black has been chosen to convey the chill of winter, but Bruegel has left traces of underpaint visible in the ice to give it a luminous quality. Dabs of white paint capture the thick snow on the ledges of the church steeple, and the snow on the steeple itself is made to stand out by a very slight darkening of the snow in the field against which it is silhouetted. The movement and attitudes of the figures and the dog are indicated very simply, with opaque dark paint and just a touch of red-brown here and there for the faces. The reflections on the ice are carefully recorded with small squiggles and dashes of paint.

1

2 *Actual size detail*

THE CORN HARVEST

1565

46½×63¼in/118×160.7cm

Oil on panel

Metropolitan Museum of Art, New York

All five of the surviving paintings of the *Months* which Bruegel produced for Niclaes Jonghelinck passed into the collection of Archduke Leopold Wilhelm in the 17th century and thence to Vienna, where only three remain today. This panel representing August with the harvesting of the corn — harvesting was also used for August in earlier Books of Hours — provides a marvellous contrast to the freezing atmosphere of January's subject, *The Hunters in the Snow* (see page 43). The heat of high summer is communicated firstly by the overall tones of rich yellows and browns, and secondly by the exhausted group gathered under the shade of the pear tree. Other workers who continue to cut the corn and stack the sheaves emphasize the harvest's relentless demand for labour. Their beautifully observed gestures were to reappear 400 years later in the peasant subjects of Jean-François Millet (opposite below).

Away to the left the landscape stretches away until it becomes lost in the hazy distance. Full of minutely observed details, it is so realistic that it is difficult to accept that it is actually imaginary, a made-up but convincing panorama. As with *The Hunters in the Snow,* the landscape and atmosphere form the real subject of the painting.

As with the first panel in the series, the design here leads the eye into the picture from the left-hand corner — a compositional layout designed to make the eye "read" the whole cycle of the Months from left to right and chronologically, as they would have been hung. The zigzag line of thick uncut corn continues towards an untidy hedgerow behind which lies an elegantly rendered church. The same church reappears at a slightly different angle in one of Bruegel's last paintings, *The Parable of the Blind* (see page 59), so it seems likely that Bruegel used an actual church as a model, although there is no known drawing of it. Down below the cornfield the countryside changes to gentle green and huddled trees beyond which lies a far field of corn in which yet more figures appear to be labouring; the loaded haywain provides a glowing colour link between the foreground and this distant paler field.

Bruegel's figures are economically depicted: he depends more on precisely observed contours than on modelling to give them reality. None of his drawings of figures supposedly done from life can be related to this painting, but since the figure of the sleeper is used again in slightly different form in *The Land of Cockaigne,* painted two years later, it is possible that there was a common source in a drawing now lost. Bruegel is also sparing in his recording of shadows. Although accurate where they do appear, they are used only here and there — just often enough to remind us of the midday heat.

The painting shows Bruegel's complete mastery of landscape painting, with the keen powers of observation and the profound knowledge of nature initiated on his journey to Italy now developed to the full. The entire scene appears natural, but the delineation of the figures, both in action and in rest, the way in which textures of trees or corn are unerringly indicated, the quality of the light and the subtlety of the palette, all reveal enormous technical skill. The picture's apparent simplicity conceals a brilliance of composition and of technique which ensures that it yields more and more to us the longer we study it. And its message is unmistakable: man is subservient to the relentless progress of the season — it is nature that dominates.

The fluid actions of the working figures in this scene contrast with the abandonment of the figures beneath the tree who are occupied with rest and refreshment. They demonstrate the ultimate purpose of the harvest — to give sustenance to humanity — both by slicing into their loaves and by reclining on the sheaves. Against the intensity that emanates from the figures, whether they are in action or repose, the landscape itself seems calmly indifferent.

JEAN FRANÇOIS MILLET
Harvesters Resting
1851-53, Museum of Fine Arts, Boston

1

1 In the middle distance a loaded cart is on its way back to the farm. The block of yellow provides a colour link between the wheatfield in the foreground and the uncut corn on the hill beyond, and contrasts with the light-toned greens around it. Clusters of trees are noted with brief lines and flecks of paint, and soft flecks are used for the window details of the turreted house set in the midst of the trees.

2 The figure bringing up provisions to the harvesters trudges between thick blocks of standing wheat. This is detailed with thin lines and dots of dark paint and emphasized by thicker dark paint to the left of the figure and at the bottom of the wheat on the right.

3 *Actual size detail* The two figures tying up the sheaves of wheat are indicated with thin paint — almost the consistency of watercolour — which shows the layer of underpaint beneath. The white cap of the bending woman contrasts with the rich deep yellow of the wheat she is tying and the pale area to each side of her. Bruegel has set off the broad washes of colour he has used for the simplified shapes of her figure and that of the man behind her with more precise strokes used for the stalks of wheat. These are accentuated in places with the point of the brush.

2

3 *Actual size detail*

THE NUMBERING AT BETHLEHEM

1566
$45^5/_8 \times 64^3/_4$ in / 116×164.5 cm
Oil on panel
Musées Royaux des Beaux-Arts, Brussels

This is one of several snow scenes produced between about 1565 and 1567 and including two versions of *The Massacre of the Innocents*. The unusual subject is taken from the Gospel according to St Luke (2:1-5). "And it came to pass in those days, that there went out a decree from Caesar Augustus, that all the world should be taxed . . . and all went to be taxed, every one into his own city. And Joseph also went up from Galilee, out of the city of Nazareth, into Judaea, unto the city of David, which is called Bethlehem (because he was of the house and lineage of David) to be taxed with Mary, his espoused wife, being great with child." The account goes on to describe the birth of Mary's first-born son who was laid in a manger because there was no room at the inn.

As with *The Procession to Calvary* (see page 35), Bruegel has given the scene a contemporary setting. A Flemish crowd is queuing up at the inn to register; an official is taking money from one man; another is noting the transaction. Pigs are being caught and killed for the travellers, people inside the inn enjoy the glow of a fire, a man opens an upper window, a pitcher and a wreath hang outside the inn. Mary and Joseph are singled out by the ass on which she rides and the ox alongside, both traditional in paintings of the Nativity. Mary has her face turned towards us while Joseph trudges by her side. He is identified by the carpenter's saw over his shoulder and by his large hat — this also appears in *The Adoration of the Kings* (see page 39).

The painting, although full of the varied activity seen in earlier works, has the greater cohesion of design noticeable in the paintings of the *Months* (see page 43 and 47). Two important diagonals are set up by the station-ary carts in the middle foreground. These are continued through the composition — one by parallel lines of houses and trees which lead to the ruined gate and fortifications of the town in the far right-hand corner, and the other by the line of figures crossing the ice, which leads to the precisely painted church in the left distance. Any implied symbolic meaning can only be guessed at, but Bruegel's deliberate positioning of things susceptible of symbolic interpretation in more than one of his religious paintings is unlikely to be pure coincidence: hidden symbolism was an important element in earlier Flemish painting. The ruined towers, which have been identified as the towers and gates of Amsterdam, might therefore refer to the time before the birth of Christ, while the little church could symbolize the era to come. Bruegel could also be making some kind of comment on the unsettled conditions in the Netherlands; in *The Massacre of the Innocents*, probably painted around the same time, Spanish soldiers are shown sacking a Flemish village. Other vivid details in *The Numbering* are the group warming themselves at an outside fire, people gathered round a tree "inn," indicated by the inn-sign swinging above, builders at work on a wooden structure and a variety of figures sporting in various ways on the ice. All are described economically, with only just as much paint as is necessary, used quite thinly and freely, noticeable in the marvellous detail of hens pecking and scratching in the foreground. The ramshackle building placed behind Mary and Joseph on a diagonal initiated by the bundle of straw in the immediate foreground has a cross on its roof, and so might represent the stable where Mary will give birth.

Bruegel's restrained palette of cream to brownish tones is enlivened only here and there by soft red. The painting has a biblical content, and the setting is a village rather than a landscape one, but the atmosphere of a particular kind of wintry day, encapsulated by the red ball of sun just setting behind the stark branches of the tallest tree, is communicated every bit as tellingly as in the paintings of the *Months*.

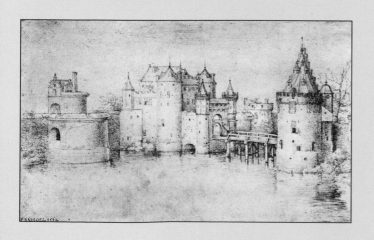

JACOB SAVERY
The Amsterdam City Gates
Museum of Fine Arts, Boston

The city gates that appear in Bruegel's painting here depicted by a contemporary.

1 *Actual size detail*

2

1 *Actual size detail* The precariousness of the two children walking on the ice is indicated by their outstretched arms and slightly splayed feet reflected by darkened areas beneath. The figures, and that child in front of them, are outlined for added emphasis, perhaps because they are relatively small. Quiet colour and precise observation of shapes gives this little group a vivid feeling of movement.

2 The cockerel with two hens, one eating, the other searching for food, are painted with thin fluent strokes over the light ground. Bruegel contrasts the stiff tail feathers of the hens with the elegant plumes of the cock, and indicates the springiness of the birds' legs and feet with delicately placed strokes. Details such as the shapes of the wings, the sharpness of the beaks, the spurs and comb of the cock, are all accurately described with a minimum of paint.

3 The turn of the ox's head towards the spectator and the highlighting of its eyes seems deliberate and may have been intended to recall the Old Testament prophecy: "The ox knows its owner and the ass its master's stall but Israel, my own people, has no knowledge, no discernment." This was understood as a foretelling of the fact that the Jews did not recognize Christ as the Messiah. Bruegel notes the ordinary activities of the villagers with his usual economy — they are unmoved by the arrival of strangers — and he successfully conveys the quality of packed snow which has been lying for some time.

3

A PEASANT WEDDING

c 1567
44⁷/₈×64¹/₈in/114×163cm
Oil on panel
Kunsthistorisches Museum, Vienna

According to Karel Van Mander, Bruegel and his friend Hans Franckert, a German merchant, used to disguise themselves as peasants and go out into the country to attend rustic celebrations of various kinds, and Bruegel "delighted in observing the droll behaviour of the peasants, how they ate, drank, danced, capered or made love, all of which he was able to reproduce cleverly and pleasantly in watercolour or oils, being equally skilled in both processes." There may be a certain amount of truth in this account, for Bruegel's vivid representation of the wedding feast suggests first-hand observation. The richly dressed man seated in the right-hand corner on an upturned churn is sometimes thought to be the painter himself, based on the man's resemblance to the engraving of Bruegel which accompanied Domenicus Lampsonius' poem about him published in 1572. But perhaps it is more likely that the figure is the local landowner; the fact that his hands are posed in the same way as those of the bride (towards the centre of the picture) provides what seems a deliberate visual link, but is unexplained. Bruegel's peasant subjects were once regarded as straightforward genre scenes, but it is now considered that they contain a degree of symbolism, like much of his work. Thus the wedding feast, in spite of the generally sympathetic portrayal of the characters, may also refer to the sin of gluttony, and the absorption of the child licking its finger seems to point up this underlying theme.

The dramatic diagonal thrust of the composition is one that is found in earlier Flemish representations of the biblical story of the Wedding Feast at Cana. Here it also provides a useful device for including the entire group in Bruegel's preferred horizontal format. Twenty guests — the maximum allowed by a decree issued by the Emperor Charles V in 1546 — are grouped around a long table backed by high-stacked hay and the last wheat sheaves of the harvest. These are pinned up with a wooden rake, while a hayfork supports the improvised cloth of honour behind the bride. Although one of the bagpipers is motionless — his longing gaze towards the food echoed by the dog scenting scraps from under the table — the painting as a whole is full of activity. Every figure is reacting to something or somebody, and the urgency felt in the two servers' brisk tread is extended by the twisting movement of the man handing out the shallow dishes of sweet rice porridge from their improvised tray. This red-hatted man, right arm reaching towards the bride, may be the groom — not otherwise identified — as it was apparently a tradition for the groom to serve the bride and her family at such a feast.

Although the white aprons of the servers and the tray of food draws the attention initially, the group in the left-hand corner provides a powerful balance. The face of the man pouring wine is painted with particular sensitivity, and the controlled urgency of his action complements the movement of the groom. The colours, textures and shapes of the pile of jugs provide a memorable still life. Apart from the creamy white of cloth and clothing, this group also contains the basic palette of the entire scene, one in which Bruegel shows an assured handling of composition, modelling and colour and an outstanding ability to record a wide variety of human expressions and poses both with sympathy and with penetrating truth.

In his biography of Bruegel, Karel Van Mander describes seeing three of the artist's paintings of peasant subjects in private collections in Amsterdam. This one, however, was acquired in 1594 by Archduke Ernst of Austria, brother of the Emperor Rudolf II and Governor of the Netherlands in 1593-95. The picture is undated, but is thought to have been painted around 1567 together with the similar-sized *Peasant Dance* which is now also in Vienna. Both compositions introduce monumental figures seen in close-up from a lower viewpoint than hitherto and are notable for the newly powerful, almost sculptural way in which the figures are modeled.

1

1 Irregular brushstrokes around the heads of the two men at the back suggest that Bruegel drew in the outlines of the figures before filling in the background colour of the wooden bench. The faces of the three wedding guests are carefully modelled in shades of cream to reddish brown with details such as lines round noses and mouths painted in with darker brown. The face of the nearest man is modelled with paler tones and small white highlights on nose, cheekbone and the centre of the eye. The three-dimensional quality of the faces of the two men in profile is emphasized by the dark tone used around eyes, noses and chins. Subtly related tones of lighter and darker grey have been used on the grey tunic of the man who is eating to convey the thickness of the material and the fullness of the raised sleeve.

2 Traces of underdrawing — on the neck of the small pitcher on the right and on the hands of the man pouring the wine, for example, and some *pentimenti* ("ghost" images formed by a lower layer of paint showing through the upper one) suggest that Bruegel drew in figures and objects on his ground before using any colour. The jugs show traces of the creamy colour also visible on floor areas beneath the darker colours which have been superimposed. The jugs have been painted with rounded, sweeping lines, as befits their shapes, and touches of white have been used to show a faint gleam on the sides and tops of some of them.

2

THE PARABLE OF THE BLIND

Signed and dated 1568

33⅞×60⅝in/86×154cm

Tempera on fine linen canvas

Museo Nazionale, Naples

The subject of the painting is taken from the Gospel according to St Matthew (15:14). Christ describes the Pharisees (the Jewish religious party who appear in the Gospels as the chief opponents of Christ) as blind leaders of the blind. "And if the blind lead the blind, both shall fall into the ditch." The parable is repeated in the Gospel according to St Luke (6:39) in the form of a question. "Can the blind lead the blind? Shall they not both fall into the ditch?" The parable is an illustration of a spiritual condition: outer physical blindness represents inner blindness, a lack of awareness of the true religion. Anyone who follows people who are already blind to the truth will, like them, fall into the ditch — be lost.

In his painting Bruegel represents the true religion by the church in the background, whose spire reaches heavenwards, out of the painting. It is placed one third across the composition in the gap between the second blind man, who is just beginning to fall — following the leader, who is already in the ditch — and the third, stumbling trustfully behind him. Bruegel presents the sightlessness of each man individually: eyeless cavities, the protruding whiteness of blind eyes, the angled heads struggling to gaze upwards to gain vision. The downward diagonal of the blind men leading to the inevitable fall contrasts with the strong verticality of the church.

Bruegel painted this work on canvas and in tempera, a medium in which the pigments are not bound with oil. This method, which he used for only a few paintings, produces a subdued colour effect due to the absorption of the pigments by the very lightly primed fine linen canvas. The paint, now very worn in places, is restrained in tone in keeping with the tragedy of the subject, and the palette is cool, with plenty of blues and greys. The way in which the six men are characterized presents an extraordinarily powerful and moving visualization of their state. Their hopeless, helpless trudge as they move painfully along, making contact with each other only by touch or through the useless security of a shared pole, is described unerringly, as are their different types of physical blindness. Their precariousness is emphasized by the narrow spit of land they walk on, placed between the watery ditch and the chalky chasm signalled in the left foreground by a frail twig.

Bruegel is stating quite unequivocally that those who are blind to true religion are without hope. But for him, what *is* the true religion? Two of the blind beggars wear rosaries, suggesting they are Catholics, as he was himself, but they too are about to fall, so to be a good Catholic is evidently not identified with spiritual awareness. In the light of all that Bruegel communicates in his work about the folly of mankind, it seems likely that he is indicating that true spirituality is out of reach for most of humanity. And although his landscape, with its verdant tree beside the church, suggests the serenity of nature that he contrasts so tellingly with human activity in his paintings of the *Months*, here the serenity is inevitably subordinated to the tragedy. The blind march on, unstoppable, away from the support of the village and its church and towards the inevitable fall. Thus the painting, one of Bruegel's last, can be seen as a sombre meditation on the fate of mankind as a whole.

This painting was in the collection of Count G. B. Masi of Parma by the 17th century. It is the largest of the paintings that Bruegel produced in 1568, the year before his death, and unlike much of his extant work it is painted in tempera on linen, rather than the more usual oil on panel. Other works by Bruegel had already portrayed the blind; a blind beggar appears in *The Battle Between* *Carnival and Lent* (see page 19), and the parable of the blind leading the blind is seen as a tiny vignette on the horizon of *The Netherlandish Proverbs* (see page 12). There were earlier precedents for the use of the parable in the work of Bosch and other Flemish artists, but Bruegel's visualization is much more agonizing, giving the six blind beggars a unique and almost unbearable reality.

1 *Actual size detail*

1 *Actual size detail* This painting was made on fine linen canvas, not Bruegel's more usual panel, and this detail shows its very worn condition. The pigments were bound with a kind of glue instead of oil, producing a more subdued colouration, and applied quite thinly, almost like watercolour, over a thin layer of priming. On the face Bruegel has used fine lines of dark paint and thin smudges to indicate shadowed areas. He has painted in tendrils of hair, teeth and slits of eyes with white paint. Dark lines have been used to emphasize the curve of the undercap, the hat and the cloak. The hand on the shoulder of the beggar shows a mixture of rather crude painting — for the thumb and little finger — and very precise detailing for the nails of the three middle fingers which are outlined and highlighted.

2 The foliage of the tree has been blocked in in dark and light greens and details of leaves painted over this in thin brown paint. Thin dark paint has also been used over the grey of the church and the orange-yellow of its roof to indicate details of stonework and tiles.

3 The pallidness of the beggar in front contrasts with the ruddy colour of his companion whose eyes are just sufficiently open to show a glimpse of white. Highlights on the cloaks are treated in a variety of ways. There is light-coloured hatching on the dark grey of the front cloak, while behind the highlights are rendered with smooth tonal changes. Tiny flicks of opaque white paint describe the crucifix and rosary around the front beggar's neck, but the trees and branches behind the figures have a translucent quality closer to true watercolour.

2

3

INDEX